Jump Rope Chant

A-B-C-D and E-F-G
I knew that when I was three.

H-I-J-K and L-M-N-O-P
Q-R-S and T-U-V
Letters make the words I see.

W-X and Y and Z
The alphabet is fun for me!

◆ **Circle the right answer.**

1. What is the poem about?

   seeing the sun   lunch time

   three toys   the alphabet

2. What is the best name for the poem?

   Letter Fun   Happy Birthday

   Time to Play   Going to School

3. What makes the words we see?

   houses   trees

   letters   me

4. What does the poem say the alphabet is?

   nice   fun

   easy   hard

Cooking Fish

Cookie is a cat. Cookie likes cooking. Cookie cooks what he likes to eat.

Cookie cooks cake. He cooks it from fish. Cookie cooks pie from fish too. Cookie even cooks cookies from fish!

◆ **Circle the right answer.**

1. What is the best name for the story?

   Real Cats   Eating Cookies   A Cat That Cooks

2. What does Cookie use to make everything he cooks?

   cookies   pie   fish   cake

3. What kind of animal is Cookie?

   a real cow   a make-believe cow

   a real cat   a make-believe cat

◆ **Circle yes or no to show which sentences are right.**

4. Real cats can cook   yes   no
5. Real cats like to eat fish.   yes   no
6. Cookie is a real cat.   yes   no

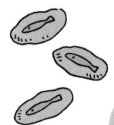

Scary Night

It was dark. It was night. Tina heard something go "Whoooo!" Tina was scared. Then, Tina heard something go "Whoooo!" again.

The window blew open. She went to close it. She saw an owl and it said, "Whoooo!" Tina was happy again.

◆ **Circle the right answer.**

1. What is the story about?

   falling asleep   reading a book

   how owls live   a scary night

2. What is the best name for the story?

   A Scary Sound   Tina's Closet

   Waking Up!   Tina's Pet

3. What did Tina hear?

   an open window   her mom

   a ghost   an owl

◆ **Write 1, 2, 3 to show how things happened.**

4. _____ The window blew open.

5. _____ Tina heard something go "Whoooo!"

6. _____ Tina saw an owl.

A Note

Mom,

I am outside. I went to the park. Adam is with me. We will be home by noon.

I love you,
Erica

◆ **Circle the right answer.**

1. What kind of writing is this?

   a funny story   a report card

   a sign   a note

2. Did Mom write the note?   yes   no
3. Did Erica write the note?   yes   no
4. Is the note to Adam?   yes   no
5. Is the note to Mom?   yes   no
6. Is Erica going to the park?   yes   no
7. Is Adam going to the park?   yes   no
8. Will Erica be home by noon?   yes   no

9. Who do you think Adam is?

   Erica's dad   Erica's teacher

   Erica's friend   Erica's goldfish

Apples

There are many kinds of apples. Apples are red. Apples are yellow. Apples are green. All apples grow on trees.

Some apples are sweet. Sweet apples taste best raw. Other apples are tart. Tart apples taste best cooked.

◆ **Circle the right answer.**

1. What is the story about?

   sweet things   apples   tart cookies

2. What does **tart** mean?

   sweet   yellow   sour   red

3. Which apples taste best raw?

   sweet apples   red apples

   tart apples   green apples

4. Which apples taste best cooked?

   sweet apples   red apples

   tart apples   green apples

5. Which kinds of apples have you eaten?

Kids' Work

Would you like a job? There are many jobs for kids. Kids can rake leaves. They can sweep sidewalks. Kids can help carry packages too.

But kids cannot drive. So there are some jobs kids cannot do now. They must wait to drive a taxi. They must wait to drive a dump truck.

◆ **Answer the questions.**

1. What is the best name for the story?

   Being a Driver   Helping Mom

   Jobs for Kids   Kids Are Too Little

2. What is something kids cannot do?

   rake leaves   sweep sidewalks

   carry packages   drive a car

3. What must kids do before they can drive?

   rake   sweep

   wait   carry

4. What work will you do when you grow up?

   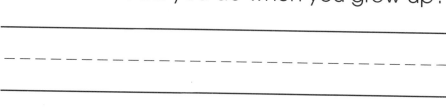

6

Classifying

The Party

The monsters had a party. They played monster games. They did monster dances. Then they cleaned up.

A monster mom looked in. She said, "Be good! Monsters are messy. Mess this room up, right now!"

◆ Circle the right answer.

1. Which one is a **monster**?

2. What is the best name for the story?

A Monster Party   Very Mean Monsters

Real Monsters   Monster Foods

3. What did the monster mom want the monsters to do?

clean up   be quiet

make a mess   go to sleep

◆ Draw a line to the word that is the opposite.

4. clean   worked

5. played   messy

Baseball Cheer

Our team is the best.
Our team never rests.

Our team really hits.
Our team never quits.

Before the games begin
We know that we will win!

Our team never rests.
Our team is the best!

◆ **Circle the right answer.**

1. What is the poem about?

   our family   our baseball team

   our school   our church

2. What is a **team**?

   a group working together to win

   a group working together to lose

3. What does our team never do?

   win   lose

   quit   hit

4. What do we know before the game?

   We will lose.   We will rest.

   We will quit.   We will win.

Leaf Mystery

The wind was blowing. Leaves fell from the trees. Many leaves were red, orange and yellow. Ty found a red leaf.

"This leaf is not real," said Ty. "Leaves are green."

But the leaf was real. What season was it?

◆ **Circle the right answer.**

1. What is the best name for the story?

   The Winter   The Red Leaf   Ty's Ride

2. Which picture shows the weather that day?

3. What did Ty find?

4. What season was it?

   spring   summer   fall

The Alien

Hal didn't like being an alien. He wanted to be a kid. He left home. He went to Earth.

Hal saw a doll by a tree. He thought it was a kid. So Hal stood very still. It was not fun.

Hal was an alien. He went back home. His mom was glad he did.

◆ **Circle the right answer.**

1. What is the story about?

   a doll   an alien   Earth

2. What is an **alien**?

   someone from another planet

   a kid who wants to be doll

3. What did Hal want to be?

   a doll   a kid   a tree

4. Which one do you think is Hal?

Scary Sunday

When Zach got up, no one was home. Where was his family? He heard a whine. It was scary.

The car was in the driveway. There was no note. He heard nothing but that whine.

They were out back! "Happy Birthday!" the family said. They were playing with Zach's new puppy!

◆ Circle the right answer.

1. What is the best name for the story?

   My First Birthday   Zach's Surprise   The Family Car

2. What did Zach hear?

   the family car   a note

   his family   a whine

◆ Draw a line to the end of each sentence.

3. When Zach woke up   a whine.

4. He heard   was in the driveway.

5. The car   no one was home.

6. "Happy Birthday!"   with Zach's new puppy.

7. They were playing   the family said.

A Thank You

Dear Grandma,

You sent such a nice surprise! Thank you for my new skates. They will look great with my new helmet. Raul says they are the best skates he's ever seen!

I love you,
Maria

◆ **Circle the right answer.**

1. What kind of writing is this?

   a note   a song

   a birthday card   a book

2. Who wrote it?

   Maria   Grandma   Mom

3. Who is it for?

   Grandma   Raul   no one

4. What will Maria wear with her skates?

Clothes

People all over the world wear clothes. Clothes keep us warm. Clothes protect us from the sun.

Some clothes are uniforms. Uniforms are special clothes. They tell us about a person's job. What uniforms do you see in your town?

◆ **Circle the right answer.**

1. What is the story about?

the sun   people   clothes   the world

2. Which one is a uniform?

3. What is one way clothes help us?

They are too big.   They keep us warm.

They are many colors.   They are called uniforms.

4. What do uniforms tell us?

special clothes   a person's job

keep us warm   someone's address

Working Dogs

Have you seen a working dog? In Alaska, dogs pull sleds over the snow. Dogsleds work better than cars in the snow.

Working dogs help people who cannot see. The dog leads the way when the owner walks outside. The dog helps the owner know where to go.

◆ **Circle the right answer.**

1. What is the story about?

   pet dogs   working dogs

   Alaska   people who cannot see

2. What work do some dogs do?

   drive a car   pull a sled   sleep

3. What other work do some dogs do?

   help people eat   help people sleep

   help people who cannot see   help people dance

4. Do dogs pull sleds?   yes   no

5. Do dogs drive cars?   yes   no

6. Do dogs help people eat?   yes   no

7. Do dogsleds work better than cars in the snow?   yes   no

The Dance

It would be the best dance!
Every dinosaur was coming.
Deeny wanted to be cool.
He got out his cool dino shoes.

Uh-oh! One shoe had a hole!
Deeny filled the hole with gum.
When the music began, Deeny
stuck to the floor! So he took off
his shoes. He was cool anyway.

◆ **Circle the right answer.**

1. What is the best name for the story?

   Deeny's Mom   Good Music

   Real Dinosaurs   Deeny's Dancing Shoes

2. What did Deeny put in his shoe?

   a dance   gum   a hole

3. What happened when Deeny started to dance?

   He put on his shoes.   He fell down.

   He stuck to the floor.   He was not cool.

4. Which one is Deeny?

A Rhyme

There was an old woman
who lived in a boot.
She fed all her children
on crackers and fruit.

When nighttime would come,
she'd say, "Off to bed! Scoot!"
And she'd play them to sleep
with a song from her flute.

◆ **Circle the right answer.**

1. What is the poem about?

   a real family   an ant family

   boots   music

2. What does **scoot** mean?

   go quickly   go slowly

3. What does the woman make with her flute?

   boots   music

   crackers   beds

◆ **Circle each picture that rhymes with scoot.**

Round Riddle

You see me at the beach. You see me in a game. I am round and filled with air. Sometimes I can bounce.

Some people use me to float. Some people use me to play catch. Some people try to sit on me! What am I?

◆ **Circle the right answer.**

1. What kind of writing is this?

   note   riddle   sign

2. What is the best name for the riddle?

   Sandy Places   Games and Work

   What Am I?   Playing in the Rain

3. What is the riddle about?

   a swimsuit   a towel

   a beach ball   a float

◆ **Circle yes or no about each sentence.**

4. It can bounce.   yes   no
5. It is always red.   yes   no
6. It is round.   yes   no
7. It can float.   yes   no

The Bug

Willie was a little car.
But everyone called him
"The Bug." He couldn't go
fast. But he was always ready.

One day when the family
had a problem, they got
in their fast car. It didn't
work. But Willie was ready.
Willie saved the day!

◆ **Circle the right answer.**

1. What is the story about?

   a family   a car   a bug

2. What is the best name for the story?

   My Family   Willie Saves the Day

   Fast Cars Are Best   How I Broke My Arm

3. What was it that Willie could not do?

   go slow   be ready

   go fast   smile

4. Which one do you think is Willie?

Whose Footprints?

One day, Mia saw footprints in her yard. Mia's mom was inside. Dad was inside too. Whose footprints were they? Was a robber coming?

Mia watched. No one came. She got scared. She told her parents. They smiled at her! "Mia, those are your footprints!" they said.

◆ Circle the right answer.

1. What is the story about?

playing in the yard   finding footprints

staying inside   smiling and talking

2. Who did Mia think made the footprints?

Mia's dad   a robber   Mia's mom

3. Who really made the footprints?

Mia   Mia's mom   a robber

◆ Draw lines to match the footprint with the one who made it.

4.

5.

An Invitation

Dear Jeremy,

We're having a party on the 4th of July. We can watch fireworks! Will you come? There will be a picnic at 6:00. Bring foods you like to eat.

See you there,
Tyrone

◆ **Circle the right answer.**

1. What kind of writing is this?

   an invitation   a song   a book

2. What kind of party is it?

   a skating party   a picnic   a birthday party

3. What should Jeremy bring?

4. Is the party for Thanksgiving?   yes   no
5. Is the party for the Fourth of July?   yes   no
6. Does the party start at 6:00?   yes   no
7. Will there be food at the party?   yes   no

Friends

Friends are people who care about you. They want you to be happy. They like to be with you.

Friends are special people who share your feelings. Friends make the world a better place.

◆ Circle the right answer.

1. What is the story about?

   places   friends

   feelings   the world

2. What is one thing friends do?

   They make the world bad.   They do not care.

   They share your feelings.   They want you to be unhappy.

◆ Draw a line to the end of each sentence.

3. Friends are people   to be happy.

4. They want you   special people.

5. They like to   who care about you.

6. Friends are   be with you.

7. Friends make the world   a better place.

The Library

Sshh...You are in a library. People read in the library. So please be quiet.

When you are here in the library, you can pick out a book. You can take the book home to read it. But remember to bring it back!

◆ **Circle the right answer.**

1. What is the story about?

   people   real things

   the library   storybooks

2. What can you do at the library?

   pick out a book   watch a show

   eat lunch   make noise

3. What should you remember to do with your book?

   be quiet   bring it back   give it away

◆ **Write 1,2,3 to show the right order.**

4. _____ Take the book home.

5. _____ Pick out a book.

6. _____ Bring it back to the library.

Mouse's House

Mouse needed a house. It did not have to be big. It did not have to be pretty. It had to be dry. It had to be warm, because winter was coming.

Mouse looked in a tree. It was not warm. Mouse looked under a leaf. It was not dry. Mouse found a boot. Mouse had a new home!

◆ Circle the right answer.

1. What is the story about?

   snow in winter   climbing a tree

   finding a house   Mouse's family

2. What did the house have to be?

   warm and pretty   big and dry

   warm and dry   big and pretty

3. Why did Mouse need a house?

   Trees are cold.   His house burned down.

   He was lost.   Winter was coming.

4. Which do you think is Mouse's new house?

Monkey Poem

Five little monkeys went to play
Out in the park one sunny day.

When Uncle Baboon said,
"On your way!"
All the little monkeys said,
"Can we stay?"

So Uncle Baboon said, "Oh, okay!
I do like to see my monkeys play."

◆ **Circle the right answer.**

1. What is the best name for the poem?

   Monkeys in the Park   The Mad Baboon

2. Who was the baboon?

   the monkeys' dad   the monkeys' uncle   the park owner

3. Was only one monkey playing?   yes   no
4. Was the baboon their mom?   yes   no
5. Did the monkeys want to stay?   yes   no
6. Did the baboon ask them to go?   yes   no
7. Did the baboon let them stay?   yes   no

Mystery Man

The stranger walked into the barn.
He was wearing a long coat and
a hat. He had hair on his chin.
He did not talk. Who was he?

Cow was afraid. Horse was afraid.
Rat went up to take a closer look.
The stranger's legs were hairy.
He had a tail. It was just Goat.
Goat was playing a trick!

◆ **Circle the right answer.**

1. What is the best name for the story?

   The Animals   On the Farm

   Stranger in the Barn   Rat Games

2. What did the stranger wear?

   a coat and shoes   a hat and coat

   a hat and pants   pants and shoes

3. Who was in the coat?

   Cow   Rat

   Horse   Goat

4. What was Goat doing?

   playing a trick   showing off his coat

   going to school   trying to hide

Sid

Sid, a snake, likes to make shapes. Sid makes a circle when he sees the sun. Sid makes an S when someone asks his name. Sid makes an egg when he sees a bird.

But Sid is too curvy. He never can make a triangle. He never can make a square.

◆ Circle the right answer.

1. What is the best name for the story?

   Real Snakes   The Sun   Sid's Shapes

2. What did Sid like to make?

   shapes   breakfast   a square

3. Sid could make a circle.   yes   no

4. Sid could make a triangle.   yes   no

5. Sid could make an S.   yes   no

◆ Draw a picture of Sid in the box below.

School Mystery

Jess got dressed, the same as every day. She put on her clothes. She put on her shoes. Jess ate her breakfast. She kissed Mom and walked to school.

No one was there! The rooms were empty. The doors were locked. "Goodness," thought Jess. "It's Saturday!"

◆ **Circle the right answer.**

1. What is the best name for the story?

   Jess Goes to School   Jess Sleeps Late

   Go to the Store   A New Home

2. Where did Jess go?

   to her house   to Grandma's   to school

3. How did Jess get there?

A Sign

Welcome to the Park!
The park is open from 9:00 to 5:00

Come see the show!
Shows are at 10:00 and 2:00.

Rules:
Do not feed the animals.
Do not litter.
Do not pick the wildflowers.
DO HAVE FUN!

◆ **Circle the right answer.**

1. What kind of writing is this?

   a sign   a song   a book

2. Where would you find this?

   at school   in the park   in church

3. When does the show start?

   10:00 and 9:00   9:00 and 5:00   10:00 and 2:00

4. What is okay for you to do at the park?

Our Flag

This is our American flag. Some people call our flag "The Stars and Stripes."

Our flag is red, white and blue. Our flag has 13 stripes. There are 7 red stripes. There are 6 white stripes. There are 50 stars. There is one star for each state in our country.

◆ **Circle the right answer.**

1. What is the story about?

   the flag   colors

   stars   stripes

2. What color are the stripes?

   50 red, 13 white   7 red, 6 white

   6 red, 7 white   13 red, 50 white

3. Why are there 50 stars?

   There are 50 states.   The stars are very small.

   There are 50 stripes too.   There are 50 stars in the sky.

4. What do some people call our flag?

   The Red and White   The Strips and Stripes

   The Stars and Stripes   The Red and Blue

The Artist

Pete is a polar bear. Pete is an artist. But everything Pete draws looks like Pete.

Pete painted a house. It was big, white and furry. Pete painted the door. It had sharp, pointy teeth. Pete painted a garden, but the flowers looked like claws. Silly Pete!

◆ **Circle the right answer.**

1. What is the best name for the story?

   Pete's Garden   Real Polar Bears   Pete the Artist

2. Is Pete a person?   yes   no

3. Is Pete a bear?   yes   no

4. Does Pete have claws?   yes   no

5. Is Pete little?   yes   no

◆ **Draw a picture Pete might draw.**

Answer Key

Page 1
1. the alphabet
2. Letter Fun
3. letters
4. fun

Page 2
1. A Cat That Cooks
2. fish
3. a make-believe cat
4. no
5. yes
6. no

Page 3
1. a scary night
2. A Scary Sound
3. an owl
4. 2
5. I
6. 3

Page 4
1. a note
2. no
3. yes
4. no
5. yes
6. yes
7. yes
8. yes
9. Erica's friend

Page 5
1. apples
2. sour
3. sweet apples
4. tart apples
5. Answers will vary.

Page 6
1. Jobs for Kids
2. drive a car
3. wait
4. Answers will vary.

Page 7
1. monster picture
2. A Monster Party
3. make a mess
4. messy
5. worked

Page 8
1. our baseball team
2. a group working together to win
3. quit
4. We will win.

Page 9
1. The Red Leaf
2. windy picture
3. red leaf picture
4. fall

Page 10
1. an alien
2. someone from another planet
3. a kid
4. alien picture

Page 11
1. Zach's Surprise
2. a whine
3. no one was home.
4. a whine.
5. was in the driveway.
6. the family said.
7. with Zach's new puppy.

Page 12
1. a note
2. Maria
3. Grandma
4. helmet picture

Page 13
1. clothes
2. uniform picture
3. They keep us warm.
4. a person's job

Page 14
1. working dogs
2. pull a sled
3. help people who cannot see
4. yes
5. no
6. no
7. yes

Page 15
1. Deeny's Dancing Shoes
2. gum
3. He stuck to the floor.
4. yellow dinosaur picture

Answer Key

Page 16
1. an ant family
2. go quickly
3. music
4. boot picture and fruit picture

Page 17
1. riddle
2. What Am I?
3. a beach ball
4. yes
5. no
6. yes
7. yes

Page 18
1. a car
2. Willie Saves the Day
3. go fast
4. yellow car picture

Page 19
1. finding footprints
2. a robber
3. Mia
4. dog
5. Mia

Page 20
1. an invitation
2. a picnic
3. food picture
4. no
5. yes
6. yes
7. yes

Page 21
1. friends
2. They share your feelings.
3. who care about you.
4. to be happy.
5. be with you.
6. special people.
7. a better place.

Page 22
1. the library
2. pick out a book
3. bring it back
4. 2
5. I
6. 3

Page 23
1. finding a house
2. warm and dry
3. Winter was coming.
4. boot picture

Page 24
1. Monkeys in the Park
2. the monkeys' uncle
3. no
4. no
5. yes
6. yes
7. yes

Page 25
1. Stranger in the Barn
2. a hat and coat
3. Goat
4. playing a trick

Page 26
1. Sid's Shapes
2. shapes
3. yes
4. no
5. yes
Answers will vary, but should show a snake.

Page 27
1. Jess Goes to School
2. to school
3. picture of walking

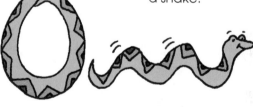

Page 28
1. a sign
2. in the park
3. 10:00 and 2:00
4. picture of a child and Dad playing ball

Page 29
1. the flag
2. 7 red, 6 white
3. There are 50 states.
4. The Stars and Stripes

Page 30
1. Pete the Artist
2. no
3. yes
4. yes
5. no
Answers will vary, but should look like something Pete would draw.